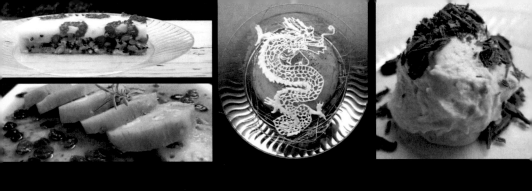

Chinese Desserts

with Classic Western Twists

Celeste Samaratunga

Chinese Desserts

with Classic Western Twists

Celeste Samaratunga

Table of Contents

Introduction

Soy Sauce, Sticky Rice, and Peking Duck seem to be ubiquitous in the world of Chinese food. However, it is little known that China is home to some of the world's most unique and versatile desserts, each with their own piece of history and place in China.

Each recipe in this book is a combination of techniques and flavors of Chinese food and Western food. We can create a fusion of Eastern and Western cultures which satisfy not only the taste buds, but also the eyes, nose, and mind.

Note about notation:
c. = cup
tbsp = tablespoon
tsp = teaspoon

Chinese
Street Food

Table of Contents

Introduction

In China's Tianjin province, the streets are paved with local specialties. One such specialty is Mahua, a sort of Chinese counterpart to a churro. It is a crispy fried bread-stick, eaten both alone and with sauces. Other specialties include red bean paste buns, caramelized hawthorne berries, and fried scorpion.

In Hong Kong, desserts such as pineapple buns and sesame balls are particularly common. These desserts are found both on the street and in restaurants.

Chinese street desserts are often sold during night markets, where the elderly and the young alike taste the freshly fried flavors of China.

Ma Hua avec Crème Chantilly

8

Ma Hua

1 c. flour

1 tbsp sugar

1 tsp salt

1 egg

1/3 c. water

icing sugar

vegetable oil for
frying

Directions

1. Mix flour, sugar, and salt together in a medium
bowl.

2. Mix egg and water together in a small bowl.

3. Pour the egg solution into the flour mixture and
stir.
   When the dough gets too thick, begin kneading it
   with your hands. Add flour when needed so the
   dough does not stick to your hands.

4. Roll out dough to about 1/8 inch thick. Slice dough
   with a pizza cutter into 1/2 inch wide strips.

5. Twist each strip to give it a rope-like shape.

6. In a medium saucepan, add vegetable oil on medium heat.

7. Once is oil is hot, add the dough strips for 30 seconds each. As strips are removed, coat with icing sugar if desired.

Crème Chantilly
with Walnuts and Black Sesame

1/2 c. heavy cream

1 tbsp sugar

1 tbsp black sesame

1/4 c. roasted walnuts

Directions

1. Mix sugar and heavy cream together in medium bowl.

2. Whisk until mixture becomes light and airy, like whipped cream.

3. Fold in sesame seeds and walnuts with a spatula.

4. Serve with Ma Hua. Serves 10.

Apple Pie Sesame Balls

Introduction

The sesame ball is a common pastry in Hong Kong's Dim Sum servings as well as during street fairs. It is made up of very chewy rice flour dough and covered in sesame seeds. They are typically filled with red bean paste, lotus root paste or black sesame paste. They date back to the Tang Dynasty, when Tang poet Wang Fanzhi mentioned it in one of his poems.

Contrary to popular belief, apple pie did not originate in the United States. Rather, it was brought to America by the British, Swedes, and Dutch in the 1800s. However, it skyrocketed in popularity in the United States while meat pies remained the more popular pastry in Western Europe. Thus, the phrase "as American as apple pie" was born.

This recipe replaces the thick, sweet red bean past filling with crunchy, tart apples. This acts in perfect harmony with the sweet, chewy outer dough. it also pairs well with the smoky flavor of the fried sesame seeds of the outside.

Apple Pie Filling

1 apple
1/3 c. water
1 tbsp sugar
1 tsp vanilla
1 tsp cinnamon

Dough

1 c. glutinous rice flour

1/4 c. brown sugar

3 tbsp water

oil for frying

Crust

1/3 c. water

1/2 c. sesame seeds

13

Filling Directions
1. Wash, peel, and dice apple into 1/2 cm cubes.

2. Mix water, sugar, vanilla, and cinnamon together in a small saucepan on medium heat.

3. Once the mixture becomes homogeneous, add apple.

4. Set filling aside to cool.

Dough Directions
1. Put the rice flour in a medium bowl. Make a well in the center of the flour.

2. Mix brown sugar and water in a small bowl and microwave on HIGH for one minute.

3. Pour brown sugar mixture into well and mix until dough is elastic and not sticky to the touch.

Assembly Directions
4. Heat oil in a large saucepan on medium heat.

5. For each sesame ball, pinch off a spherical piece of dough roughly 2 cm in diameter and flatten into a circle roughly 5 cm in diameter.

6. Place 3/4 teaspoon of filling into circle of dough. Seal the filling in the dough to make a spherical shape.

7. Put 1/3 cup water into small bowl. Put sesame seeds in another small bowl.

8. Dip all sides of each ball into water. Immediately roll ball in sesame seeds, so the sesame seeds completely cover ball.

9. Fry in hot oil for 2-3 mins. Makes 12 sesame balls.14

15

Table of Contents

Oolong-Lotus Semifreddo

Ingredients

3/4 c. heavy cream
3/4 c. sugar
2 eggs
1/2 c. oolong tea
1 lotus root, diced
dark chocolate, for garnish

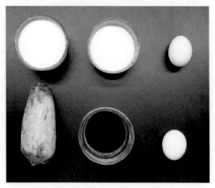

Directions

1. Separate eggs. Put egg yolks and 1/4 c. sugar in a large bowl. Mix well.

2. Heat tea and lotus root in a large saucepan until boiling.

3. Pour tea into egg yolks through a sieve (to catch lotus chunks) while mixing vigorously so as not to cook the egg yolks.

4. Pour mixture back to saucepan and heat until the mixture is thick enough to coat the back of a spoon. Pour into medium bowl and allow to chill in fridge for one hour.

5. In another medium saucepan simmer water on medium heat.

6. In a medium bowl, add two egg whites and 1/4 + 2 tbsp sugar. Mix with whisk.

7. Place the medium bowl over the saucepan with the water and whisk vigorously for 5 minutes.

19

8. Take off heat and whisk until the consistency of meringue.

9. In a large bowl, whisk heavy cream and remaining sugar until consistency of whipped cream.

10. Fold in tea mixture.

11. Fold in meringue.

12. Chill bowl in freezer for 3-5 hours.

13. To serve, take out a scoop with an ice cream scooper and garnish with chocolate.

Ginger Curd Crème Brûlée

with Black Sesame Lace Cookies

Ginger curd is a common Chinese treat, consisting of milk curdled only with ginger. It is light, not very sweet, and is pungent with ginger.

In contrast, crème brûlée is a heavy, rich French dessert which perfectly compliments the ginger curd. Usually, sugar is sprinkled on top and brûléed with a blow torch. However, in this recipe, this would simply burn the curd. This recipe calls for a crunchy cookie on top as a substitute.

Crème Brûlée

2 egg yolks
1/4 c. sugar
2 tsp vanilla
1/2 c. heavy cream
1/4 c. skim milk

Ginger Curd

3/4 c. whole milk
2 tsp fresh ginger juice
1 tbsp sugar

Black Sesame Lace Cookies Adapted from Joanne Chang's *Flour*

2 tbsp butter
2 tbsp sugar
2 tbsp brown sugar
2 tbsp flour
1 tbsp clementine juice
1 tbsp black sesame

Crème Brûlée Directions

1. Heat cream, milk and 2 tbsp sugar in medium saucepan until just about to boil.

2. Stir egg yolks and remaining sugar in a large bowl.

3. Pour cream mixture into egg mixture while whisking egg mixture vigorously so as not to cook the eggs.

4. Stir in vanilla.

5. Pour mixture equally into three ramekins.

23

6. Put ramekins in a dish. Fill dish with boiling water, so the water reaches half the height of the ramekins.

7. Bake at 325 degrees Fahrenheit for 40-50 minutes.

8. Take out and let look for 3 hours.

Ginger Curd Directions
1. Heat milk and sugar in a small bowl in the microwave on HIGH for one minute. Stir.

2. Pour ginger juice into milk. Give bowl a quick swirl.

3. Without stirring, immediately pour into ramekins equally on top of the crème brûlée.

4. Let chill in refrigerator for 2 hours.

Lace Cookie Directions
1. Mix all ingredients together. The dough will be paste-like.

2. In rounded teaspoons, drop dough onto a lined baking sheet. Leave 2 inches around each cookie. They spread quite a bit.

3. Bake at 350 degrees Fahrenheit for 16-18 minutes.

4. Immediately after taking out of oven, use a knife to cut cookies into the size of the ramekins.

5. Let cool, and place a cookie on top of ginger curd in each ramekin. Serves 3.

Raspberry - Coconut Bars

with Tapioca Bubbles

Crust

1/2 c. water
1/2 c. sugar
1/4 c. maple syrup
1 c. sunflower seeds, roasted
3 tbsp black sesame, roasted
2 tsp salt

Directions

1. Line the bottom of a 9x9 square dish with parchment paper.

2. Mix water, sugar, and maple syrup in a medium saucepan over high heat.

3. When mixture reaches 140 degrees Fahrenheit, stir in sunflower seeds, black sesame seeds, and salt.

4. Pour mixture into square dish.

5. Set aside to cool.

Tapioca Bubbles

1/4 c. tapioca pearls
1 c. water
1/4 c. frozen blueberries

Directions

1. Heat water and blueberries in a medium saucepan on low-medium heat until boiling.

2. Add tapioca pearls.

3. Let simmer for 30-40 minutes until pearls are chewy.

4. Pour a layer of pearls on top of crust.

Coconut Bars

3/4 c. coconut milk
1/4 c. skim milk
1/4 c. sugar
4 tbsp cold water
2 tbsp gelatin
1 pint raspberries

Directions

1. Heat coconut milk, skim milk, and sugar in a large saucepan on medium heat.

2. Put gelatin into cold water and let rest for 3-5 minutes.

3. When milk mixture is just about to boil, take off heat and let cool for 3-5 minutes.

4. Pour gelatin mixture into milk mixture. Stir well.

5. Pour mixture into dish with the tapioca pearls and crust.

6. Place Raspberries in the jelly so part of the raspberry sticks out. Let cool in refrigerator for 4-6 hours.

7. Use knife to carefully cut off tops of raspberries to reveal a cross-section that looks like a flower on top of bar. Cut into bars. Serves 10.

Dragonfruit Clafoutis

with Dried Cranberries

Ingredients

1 14-oz can sweetened condensed milk

1/2 c. heavy cream

2 tbsp flour

2 tsp vanilla

2 eggs

1 dragonfruit, peeled & diced

3 tbsp dried cranberries

icing sugar (for dusting)

rosemary (for garnish)

Directions

1. Scatter dragonfruit on the bottom of two 4-inch dishes or one 9-inch dish.

2. Combine heavy cream, flour, vanilla, and eggs in a medium bowl. Pour on top of dragonfruit.

3. Scatter dried cranberries over the mixture.

4. Bake at 350 degrees Fahrenheit for 35-40 minutes.

5. Let Cool.

6. Dust with icing sugar and garnish with a sprig of rosemary.

Elegant Dishes

Table of Contents

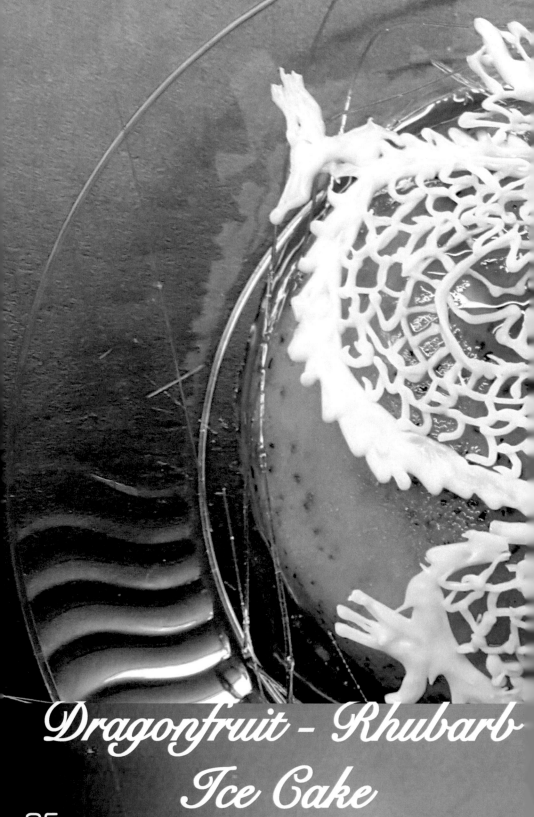

Dragonfruit - Rhubarb
Ice Cake

Ingredients
1/2 c. white chocolate chips
1 6-inch stalk of rhubarb, diced
1 stalk of lemongrass
1 dragonfruit, peeled & diced
1/2 c. sugar
1/2 c. water

Directions
1. Heat white chocolate in a small bowl for 20 seconds in the microwave and stir. Repeat two more times.

2. Cut a very small corner off of a ziploc bag and put chocolate inside of bag.

3. Place a piece of parchment paper over template on page 38. Use template to pipe a dragon out of white chocolate.

4. Stir rest of ingredients together in a large saucepan. Cook on medium heat for 20 minutes.

5. Pour mixture through sieve into hemisphere molds.

6. Freeze for 5 hours.

7. Unmold and place dragon over ice cake.

38

Chinese Fondant Cutting

on Milk Chocolate Base

40

Chinese Paper-Cutting is a traditional Chinese art-form in which a knife is used to cut intricate designs out of paper. Here, we will be cutting intricate designs out of fondant instead and lay them on a base of chocolate for stability. This decoration looks amazing on cakes and is a great way to personalize any dessert.

Ingredients
1/2 c. dark chocolate, tempered
2 ounces fondant
cornstarch
1 tsp water
food coloring, optional

Method
1. Find or make a template out of paper of the design that you would like to cut out.

2. Roll out fondant into the size that you want your fondant cut-out to be. It should be about 1/8 inch thick.

3. Dust both sides of fondant heavily with cornstarch.

4. Place fondant on cutting board. Place template over fondant.

5. Attach template to fondant with a little water on places that will be cut out.

6. Use a knife to cut out the design with guidance from the template.

7. Carefully take template off of fondant.

Chocolate Base

1. Heat chocolate in microwave for 20 seconds. Stir. Repeat two more times.

2. Pour melted chocolate on parchment paper, and spread into roughly the same size as the fondant cutout.

3. Let harden for 2 minutes.

Assembly

1. Place fondant cut-out over chocolate.

2. Let chocolate fully harden for 4 minutes more.

3. Paint fondant cut-out with food-coloring if desired.

Five - Spice Sachertorte

The Austrian Sachertorte is one of the most famous Viennese desserts. It is a rich dark chocolate sponge cake glazed apricot jam and chocolate icing.

Chinese five-spice is a mixture of equal amounts of star anise, cloves, Chinese cinnamon, Sichuan pepper, and fennel. It is usually used for seasoning meat, but it adds a nice touch to the classic Sachertorte.

This recipe is filled with apricot jam instead of glazed with it, so that every bite of chocolate-spice flavor can be eaten with the tartness of the jam.

Ingredients
1 oz bittersweet chocolate
2 tbsp butter, softened
1/4 c. icing sugar
2 egg yolks
1 tsp vanilla
2 egg whites
2 tbsp sugar
1/4 c. flour
1 tsp Chinese five-spice
2 tbsp apricot jam
1 tsp icing sugar, for garnish

Directions

1. Preheat oven to 400 degrees Fahrenheit. Grease two ramekins with vegetable oil.

2. Melt chocolate in microwave.

3. Whisk together butter and icing sugar.

4. Vigorously whisk in egg yolks until mixture is a pale yellow.

5. Add melted chocolate and vanilla.

6. With a clean whisk, whisk egg whites and granulated sugar together until soft peaks form.

7. Fold egg yolk mixture into egg white mixture.

8. Fold in flour and Chinese five-spice.

8. Pour evenly into the two ramekins.

9. Bake for 40 minutes.

10. Let cool.

11. Use a knife to cut bottom out of each cake.

12. Fill with apricot jam.

13. Place the bottom back into the cake. Makes 2.

14. Plate and garnish with icing sugar.

Stuffed Lotus Root
with Rosemary-Mint Sticky Rice

Every part of the lotus plant is used in Chinese cuisine, be it for tea or for curries. Lotus root is a staple due to its high dietary fiber and exceptional levels of vitamins B and C. Stuffed lotus root is found as both an appetizer and a dessert in much of Southern China. Usually, the lotus is stuffed with sticky rice and flavored with honey and osmanthus syrup.

Since the mid-20th century, fresh herbs have been an essential in French cuisine, replacing commonplace heavy dishes, such as roux. Herbs are found particularly in French Provencal cuisine in entrées such as aïoli and ratatouille.

This recipe combines the fresh herbs of France with the stuffed lotus root of China to create a subtle blend between the east and the west. Instead of osmanthus and honey, this lotus root is infused with rosemary and mint to bring a fresh twist to the classic Chinese dish.

47

Stuffed Lotus Root

2 c. water
1 c. raw sticky rice, rinsed*
1 sprig of rosemary
3 mint leaves
2 lotus roots, washed
1 tbsp dried cranberries
2 tbsp sugar
8-10 toothpicks

Sauce

2 c. water
2 tbsp sugar
2 tbsp brown sugar
2 tbsp dried cranberries

Filling Directions

1. Put water, rice, rosemary, and mint into a small saucepan. Stir with wooden spoon, then close with saucepan lid. Let boil on medium heat for 25-30 minutes.

2. While rice is boiling, peel lotus roots. Cut top off each lotus root. Set aside.

3. After rice is done boiling, stir 1 tbsp dried cranberries and 2 tbsp sugar into the rice.

4. Use chopsticks to fill holes in lotus root with rice mixture.

5. Close lotus root with lotus root top. Fasten the two parts of the lotus root together with 4-5 toothpicks. Repeat for second lotus root.

49

Sauce Directions

1. Mix all sauce ingredients together in a medium saucepan over medium heat.

2. When the sauce begins to simmer, add the two lotus roots.

3. Leave the two lotus roots to simmer for 2 hours.

4. Let lotus roots cool, then slice and plate them, pouring the sauce over them. Serves 8.

*If you don't have sticky rice, any rice will work well. However, you must cook the rice for 40 minutes in 2 1/2 cups of water so that it has a similar texture to sticky rice.

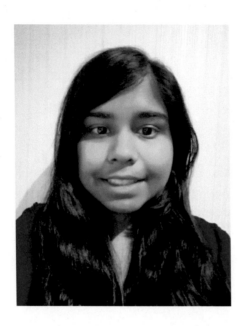

About the Author

Celeste Samaratunga resides in the United States and has
been dessert blogging ever since she was 14, running the
blog *Drizzled With Chocolate.* She has worked under
Executive Chef Rohan Fernandopulle of "*Le Club des
L'association gastronomique la plus exclusive au monde*"
fame at the industrial pastry kitchen of Water's Edge
Restaurant in Colombo, Sri Lanka.

Her passionate energy extends far beyond the pastry bag.
She has been learning Mandarin Chinese for nearly half a
decade and has competed in the international Chinese
Bridge Proficiency Competition. This brought her to
Beijing, Shanghai, Hangzhou, and Kunming where she
tasted street food and homemade food alike, inspiring her to
share her loves of both baking and Mandarin with others.